The HUB of
The MIRACLE

The HUB of The MIRACLE

by

Sallie Bingham

SANTA FE

© 2006 by Sallie Bingham. All rights reserved.

No part of this book may be reproduced in any form or by any electronic or mechanical means including information storage and retrieval systems without permission in writing from the publisher, except by a reviewer who may quote brief passages in a review.

Sunstone books may be purchased for educational, business, or sales promotional use. For information please write: Special Markets Department, Sunstone Press, P.O. Box 2321, Santa Fe, New Mexico 87504-2321.

Library of Congress Cataloging-in-Publication Data

Bingham, Sallie.
  The hub of the miracle : poems / by Sallie Bingham.
     p. cm.
  ISBN 0-86534-480-9 (pbk. : alk. paper)
  I. Title.

PS3552.I5H83 2006
811'.54—dc22
                                        2005033872

WWW.SUNSTONEPRESS.COM
SUNSTONE PRESS / POST OFFICE BOX 2321 / SANTA FE, NM 87504-2321 /USA
(505) 988-4418 / ORDERS ONLY (800) 243-5644 / FAX (505) 988-1025

"I will be leaning in like a spoke to the hub, the dense orb that is all of us."

—Mary Oliver

For Peg and Frank Steele

CONTENTS

INTRODUCTION / 13

1 / IN MOURNING / 17

    The Prophet is Never Welcome in Her Own Country / 19
    Iron Shield / 20
    Funeral Meats / 22
    The Fire's Moment / 24
    Lighting the Stove / 26
    Maybe That's the Answer / 27

2 / IN WINTER / 29

    Early December / 31
    Indigo / 32
    Work / 33
    Writing Two Poems Every Day / 34
    Touch is the Miracle / 36

3 / WHAT THE STOVE SAYS

    Lid / 39
    M.A. Godin's Stove / 40
    Pail of Pinecones / 42
    Such Good Timber / 43
    The Stove Pipe Speaks / 44
    Nine Degrees: A Woman Banks A Fire / 46
    Three Fires / 48

4 / AFTER THREE MARRIAGES / 49

Growing Up with Legends / 51
After Three Marriages / 52
After Three Weddings / 54
Last Child / 56
Not for Me the Long Knowing / 57
A Way to Dance / 58
The Massage / 60
Seventeen: The Pink Dress / 61
First Poem / 62
Learning to Skate / 64
And You Were There / 66
Where He's Staying / 68
Telling Tales / 70
Five / 71
Mother Love / 72
Sannyasa / 73

5 / DAILY NEWS / 75

    Chechnya / 77
    I Cannot Do / 78
    Walk / 79
    The Tree that Grows in the Center of the World / 80
    Shearing Him / 81
    Daily News / 82
    Guaco / 83
    Make-Work / 84
    Sleeping in Pearls / 85
    Losing the Sextant / 86
    Crossing the Border / 87
    The Child Who / 88
    February: Lilies of the Valley / 89
    Event / 90
    The Old Burn / 92
    Bill Cody's Wild West Show / 93
    Sunday Afternoon Concert / 96
    Now We Are Thirty / 98
    Death of Medicine Wheel / 100
    Sisters-In-Law / 102

INTRODUCTION

I grew up with poetry, which my father defined as something far different from, and far superior to, verse. One of my first books was a now-battered copy of *Palgrave's Golden Treasury*, which I am sure no one would give to a child today. It contained great swatches of Shakespeare and the romantic poets, to all of whom I gave my considered attention, scrawling sometimes-dismaying comments in the margins. And, when I was unruly, or perceived to be, I was allowed to memorize poems to escape whippings. I still remember sections of "The Rhyme of the Ancient Mariner" and "The Wreak of the Schooner Hesperus"—only long poems earned a reprieve from belt or slipper.

Such an education might have made me hate poetry but instead I became its ally as it became mine. No other form of literature, even the prose I have written for years, has earned me a similar reprieve from just or unjust punishment. And so I keep in my heart a love, even a passion, for poetry (and not verse), which is finally finding its home in my first book, *The Hub of the Miracle*.

The title comes from a poem by Mary Oliver who gave me permission to use it even though we have both forgotten which of her poems contains the line. Her poems about the deep stillnesses she finds in nature, stillnesses that often contain an implicit threat, have given me the courage to put down my own notes on quiet and the peril it contains. I love simplicity in poetry but find that it has taken me a long while to claim simplicity—which is never simple—as my own. I find my words on walks, in woods, in arroyos here in the southwest, or in those moments of sometimes terrifying clarity that come in the midst of the most mundane activity.

After my father died, my mother in her grief was sleepless, and found relief in quoting parts of the Shakespeare sonnet they had both loved: "Let me not to the marriage of true minds." Again, poetry offered salvation.

Perhaps a few lines from this book may help a sleepless reader through the long dark hours.

—Sallie Bingham
Santa Fe

The HUB of The MIRACLE

1
IN MOURNING

THE PROPHET IS NEVER WELCOME IN HER OWN COUNTRY

Do you see her at day's end creeping
from tree to tree? Her eye is on you—
strange orb, pricked by the setting

sun. Has your darkness caught
her dangerous gleam? She hunts you
as the starving coyote in a dry
winter hunts the quivering mouse,

flayed by moonlight under a dead
leaf; and the eye that marks the sparrow
marks her lunge at your throat. Beware

the woods, then, lock your door
against the stealthy moonlight; she is
still there, behind the naked November

trees, she is still waiting to heap
in your ears the words you will hear
when you are dying, that will close your senses

like sand.

IRON SHIELD

Bury him next to the crumbling
      edge of his father's
          coffin: two men, both
young. They meet now as equals,
      partakers of destruction,
          deep drinkers
of death. And we—the women—begin
          once more
our mourning, tear hair, grind

teeth, light the ritual bonfire,
      bathe in hot ash,
          while Truth, hideous hag,
squats on her tripod, sees
      the silk time when they wore
          our favors,
when we gave them the iron shield.
          How we cheered
them, then, stirred to ecstasy

by the clashing of metal.
      How we stretched to
          hear the crunch of bones,
and sniffing delicately
      drew in the aphrodisiac
          stench of new blood.
Cease, oh hag,
      your murderous
remembering! For now we are mourning,

    now we are wailing, "Oh,
            the brilliance, oh—"
                while under the cooling
ashes of their funeral
            pyres, the dull, dark
            edge of
the iron shield appears,

and we are caryatids,
            once more, exquisitely
            draped, bearing their
coffins on our beautiful
            shoulders.

FUNERAL MEATS

We will gather, touching hands,
we will eat what's provided:
cake, meat, sundry casseroles,
we will say to each other,
it will never happen again.
Death's shut like a shop.

There are little boys now
playing with blocks who will
play later in their fathers'
graves, there are girls already

preparing their eyes for tears;
and Death, that old wiseacre, gums
a bit of cheese with the best
of us, biding his time.

We will forget in gardens,
in woods, in houses, we'll
grow satisfied again with
our places, will lose
our shadows, or bleach them.

Death knows. He doesn't resent
our forgetting: kings
have peasants, too, who dance
in the wine presses. He will drink
our juices, flashing eye teeth
in that dark dawn when alone

(where are the cakes, where are the casseroles?)
we wake to the touch of his hand,
not cold, warm, rather, familiar
as a child's mitten, and know
his claim, like pride's, is immutable.

THE FIRE'S MOMENT

After the kindling,
the match,
crushed pages,

after the first roar,
the fire has
its moment,

dying, by degrees,
quietly,
to red coals—

a moment when life
flickers. The heart
pumps, once again,

against its destroyer,
the lungs expand,
hope flows

along the veins.
Then, quietly,
very quietly,

the moment
passes. Flame
and heat die.

But this fire is not for
the boy convulsing
on a silk couch;

this flame's
redeemable—
oh easily!

Another handful
of kindling, pages
crumpled, a helpful

second match.
Now, the roar!
Brief, but satisfying.

For the boy, though—
the man—no match is
sufficient. He wishes

death, has wished
it for a long time.

Some fires have
no moment.

LIGHTING THE STOVE

Piñon won't catch
easily. Bent limbs,
thin as a cripple's,
resist.

Pinecones, or three
orange sticks of
greasewood help
a little.

Death's like that:
a refusal to kindle.
We pile on hope,
entreaties.

He won't rise
unless, as to Lazarus,
one comes whose touch
is fire.

MAYBE THAT'S THE ANSWER

Maybe that's the answer: to wait
for the incense stick to go out
by itself, releasing its sweet
plume; for the logs to catch,
unaided; for my dog to return,
uncalled, from snuffling and sipping
the snow; for these tears to pass.

But the waiting that allowed
two brothers to die,
one after the other; that waiting
so long it blotted memory
until their nephew's death:

what voice, raised, what hand,
lifted, could have so sped time
clocks lost the space reserved
for tragedy? Cherish that blank

unmeasured slot between what
comes, silently, on its own feet
and what pads after.

2
IN
WINTER

EARLY DECEMBER

The start of winter takes away
what can't last, can't stand the cold:
the old dancer, thin as a fragment
of fingernail, the young man wreathed
in what we take for glory; early December

draws them, at the witching hour,
when snow pours down. They are spared
January's iron jaw, February's
faulty promises, blow-hard March's

pretenses. The earth's not frozen yet.
Slip them in. Their deep graves smell
of summer damp and roots, fetid
mild reek of quick decay.

INDIGO

Indigo answers the truckers' calls
on her own CB, its battery pack parked
        on her kitchen table. "They get frisky,"
        she says, "til I tell them I'm 92."

Between baking her pies in the morning,
between naps in the afternoon,
        she guides them in
           to Central Steel. At night

she leaves her CB on for the lost
ones, wandering late on the interstate.
        Once, she had a son
        who slipped off the edge

of the map. She doesn't think of him
when her CB crackles, when another voice
        breaks the thin skin
        of her calm. All directions
she knows, lead to the same place.

WORK

> "I should have been a plumber."
> —Einstein

Something in my heart wants work,
just the simple kind, not words: carrying
split logs down from the shed to add
to the hard round log by the door—
givers to resisters, the partial
to the whole; or, in cold morning sun,
bringing water to the patient fern,
who bides its time, hiding its fiddleheads
under its leafy wings; or picking dry yellow
leaves off the unblooming geraniums
that are also waiting for something.

Is it spring? Rosemary pushing its needles
through the last snow? Or some towering
moment that makes dailiness glow
for an instant before putting it out?

We are the only ones who wait.
It's a talent we have, a gift for endless
anticipation. If my days were spent
hauling wood and watering ferns,
would I lie down more easily at the end?

WRITING TWO POEMS EVERY DAY
For Emily Dickinson

It came on her
        in the spring: dandelions
        in new grass, already
        seeding; bread to be set
to rise,

the kettle filled up,
        again, set on the stove,
        again, cups laid out.
        Water, and words
flow like the dammed creek

at the foot of the garden.
        The dam's choked
        with wild cress: see
        to it! Each small green
leaf a word lost to the wind.

There's mending, too,
        a winter's socks with holes
        in heels and toes. Do words
        spin a web clear as a darner's
net, that fills with even stitches—

or catch the bright
        serviceable memories to fill
        a brother's pail? Reason not
        the need; all words are closed,
finally, like pens in a flannel pocket,

staining it; and at day's end—
        spring, or not spring—hands lie down
        on knees, in laps, knowing only
        that labor—some sort of saving work—
                is done.

TOUCH IS THE MIRACLE

The young man in the white t-shirt holding out his hand
                for the first step
                of the quickstep
is the young man I bore many years ago,

half-knowing; his round, brown shoulder ploughed me
                in that sleep
                on the delivery table,
closer to death than to dreaming. Where lie the roots

of his daring, his quick breath as we begin to dance?
                Not in the moment
                of fatal conception,
not in this late learning, but in the melting place of

action and desire where the child's cry and the beat
                of the quickstep
                are melded,
and even on our deathbeds, kisses glide.

3
WHAT THE STOVE SAYS

LID

It stuck
its beak in my thumb pad
through the glove.

I felt, but didn't know:
a creature come to sit
on the stove top? Some malicious

bird? The road to apprehension
is long. Too long. Now the
round red blister lifts

from the end of my thumb.
It knew, from the start.

M.A. GODIN'S STOVE

A man in a hat
        made my stove
in France,
        a long time
ago,

numbered it
        inside the lid.

In dreams he saw
        the curly frame
                of the roaring door,

its isinglass
        window,
                steel stem

that rattles down
        dead coals.

Waking, he saw
        serviceable top,
                a place to heat

a pot
to boiling.

Dreams don't count
>for much, yet M.A.
>>Godin's frame,

the elegant setting
>he wrought
>>for the fire's mad eye

touches me more.

PAIL OF PINECONES

Who matched
the underlip of the pinecones
to the adobe lining
of the pail?

And mashed
its edge in,
speckling black tin
with almost pink

mud of the earth,
blended,
valueless
til applied?

Two holes,
once for a handle,
baleful as eyes
look out.

What is beauty
but neglect
and chance?

SUCH GOOD TIMBER

Such good timber, soft as balsa—
the boy's delicate, particular airplanes,
                strung from strings;
where are those beautiful hands?

As the timber, burning, casts
a good ash, log-shaped, as the
                pieces of planes
left behind their pattern, pinecones

in the snow carve marks
                larger than they,
as though fragility weighs

where branches, stones
leave only their shapes
                no more. So
the boy's hands, long ago, carved
their shapes in the air,

leaving larger spaces
                in memory and imagination.

THE STOVE PIPE SPEAKS

    At my side
            stands
    a square
            stone.

    Not flat like
            all
    the others,
            placed

    rhythmic in my
            chimney,
    but square as
            a box.

    This stone
    you can move.

    Inside's a
            dark
    place where
            leaks,

    fissures, gape
            little
    mouths, cracks
            yawn.

Here enters
        cool
air, here
        opens

an invitation.
        Place
your hand
        inside:

treasure
is space.

NINE DEGREES: A WOMAN BANKS THE FIRE
For Will

Some place
        in a past I don't remember
a woman banks
        the fire, nesting
live coals in dead ashes,
        thinking their lives depend on it:

husband,
        son. Half-cured cow hides,
store-boughten
        blankets won't warm the night,
but coals, live as eyes,

glare through the stove door
        from light to light
heating their precious sleep.

So she thinks.
        There's snow, this morning,
on the Colorado border,
        Antonito's planked
with white: my life, alone,
        depends on it.

And my son's
        green wood bench,
by the kitchen door, recalls,
        though haltingly,
my time of need, my wish
        endlessly to provide.

The temperature's stuck
         in the gauge, the sun
won't raise it any time today,
         the banked fire can't pull
that needle up; but some place

my son
         still sleeps under the stove's
watching, some place live coals
         preserve themselves in ashes,
and our fragile lives go on.

THREE FIRES

    In winter
        morning wind blurts
through my bedroom
        windows, chills my sheets,
ruffles my sleeping hair.

Even the first
        log flaring on the hearth
can't tame this wind,
        warm these sheets
or settle my hair.

Downstairs, the stove
        fires up, eager
to fight the house's
        chill, square
of frozen air the night laid.

And then, in the secret place
        where I work alone
the third fire flares,
        a signal fire, this one,
lighting the way to peace.

4
AFTER THREE MARRIAGES

"Paradise had its laws."
—Sharon Olds

GROWING UP WITH LEGENDS

> "And now this is 'an inheritance'"
> —Seamus Heaney

Behind the trap door that is the past, their faces
are always waiting, propped on tops that,
alone, are strange: dancer's broad shoulders,
brocade of the wife of the ambassador,
debutante daughter's white satin bow,
      bride's dimity.

No one tells their stories, no one needs to know them,
they are told by the hands, the feet, the eyes
of those who are here now, who inhabit
what they will never know: the heart
squeaking like a cornered rat under the lace dress—
      the grief of women.

Words are plain and poor. Let images reign
as a new generation comes to gaze on these
shadows: how one brought money, one, talent,
one, beauty—and left them on these alters
with virginity, maidenhood, bride hopes,
      age which

behind the trap door that is the past glows
with the thousand eyes of the Hindu goddess
      who alone
          owns us all.

AFTER THREE MARRIAGES

Somehow, it was never enough,
and yet—how to say it?—
the trying, though doomed, was all:
web-veil I wore for the illicit trip
to the beach, sunsuits I packed for
the children on licit trips, later—

but always, at one end of the night
or the other, rasp of palm trees, undeterred,

or the little ships of sighs that sailed,
now and then, on my husbands' renouncing.
Not one of them a crier. Nor was I. There's
a crisp manner of despair I like even now
when winning and losing and starting again
are over: the child's porridge bowl knocked

to the floor, Jack and Jill tumbling,
the kitchen with its bright light blotted,

the stranded highchair, its tray up, stained
sheets of the crib, the bassinet, gone
to some landfill. There's no marriage
without children, no children without
marriage; they are born that we, together,
may do them harm. Even now

I ride high hopes, I believe in palm
rasps and a certain angle of light,

in the cruel necessities that seal us,
the cruel necessities that tear us apart.

AFTER THREE WEDDINGS

The first one was the right kind: cream
satin smooth as the inside of my elbow,
veil conferred by generations of
sorrowful women who knew how to smile,
strangers in small hats and fur tippets
leaning into the aisle. Tears, not music,
accompanied me, although that was not
my plan, and my father's hand
on my long kid glove said, "This
is the way." To my sorrow, I knew
better, had already seen the glare
of my mother's shelved despondency,
laid away with lavender sachets
and monogrammed linen sheets. "I'll
never understand you," she said,
having taught me lessons I refused

to believe. At the judge's, the second
time, such faith was not needed. My
first son slept in his sailor suit
on a hard bench, his nurse applauded,
I saw her belief sparkle like mica
in the dull, savorless words. There
was no blessing. But fruit comes
even when spring blossoms are
nipped—sons, with disillusionment,
sweet as bees. Do not dare to disturb
the quiet square at the top of the stairs
where they sleep, breathing my dreams. Every
night I arrange them carefully in the feathery
nest of my discontent, I hold them there
forever, wrapped in my leaves, or at least

for a few more years. The robin is dauntless,
patrolling the wet yard for worms, but I know,

finally, only how to let go. Wreckage passes,
the sea is untouched and goes on
rolling timbers. The third time the judge is
a friend, he gives me an orchid to pin
on my suit, and I am suddenly returned
to the great feasts of my childhood, where
passion—it seemed to me—roared. The house
is full of children, now, they remain

fiercely unrelated, they insist on it, and
in their flattened eyes I see reflected our
eternal bitterness. There is no tie that binds
in the face of a boy's anguish, the tears
he has not yet learned to hide. On the kitchen

table, or starting up in the dead of night
when for all their raging they are breathing
steadily around me, I write, I say
those final words: no more. The clock
falls from the wall, spilling springs,
the front door drifts open, and the air,
the sharp air I thought I'd lost forever
slides its knife-edge in.

LAST CHILD

Sitting in the rocker in the narrow dark room
behind the kitchen, I put him to my breast—
favorite place, favorite time; no one will
come here. Once an Irish girl wept on this
low bed, once a fancy French girl lured her
lover in, but now it is only a grey cell
for life's spark, the baby I am making,
now, as I made him six months ago
in my belly. My milk builds him, cell
by cell, as my blood built him, then;
he sucks masterfully, his left hand beating
a mild tattoo on my breast, his blue eyes
searching my face. This is the look I
wanted and never found, for all lovers
are distracted, they have other things
to look at; I did not build them cell
by cell. In time, I know, I'll have to
wean him, my rock-hard breasts leaking
when, enraged, he cries and bats away
the bottle, leaking dim white tears for his
lover's stare that will not come again.

NOT FOR ME THE LONG KNOWING
For Sharon Olds

Not for me the long knowing, two
bodies paired for years losing their
skins to each other, trading bone for bone—
and the finer points, those hidden flaps
of flesh only time, perhaps, can honor.

I live instead in connections so brief
disillusion can't subsist there: the brushed
kiss after the shared meal, the food
"not so good," hands touching over
the check, two right hands, both

equally determined. Those are nails
I won't see cut, the penitent bend
of the body over the toes. Yet there's
a strange, unwilled knowing that
warns away from longer touching,

a silence that speaks only
in small words: enough, it says,
enough; this is material sufficient
for your making.

A WAY TO DANCE

A woman dancing in a stranger's
arms sees herself in the mirror-
one flash-and her mouth's
working, gumming, jawing
the hard cud of her past. Someone

said, No, then, for the first and last
time, someone said, Not those legs,
that face, that hair, that seed-
soul clenched between your teeth. Now
at last in the arms of a stranger,

she gums it in waltz time, one,
two, three, she grinds her
jaws to the Tango, sliding
her feet away from his pants leg,
jawing to the Jitterbug the hard,

sour lump of the past. Spit it
out, she thinks, it has lost
all savor, you'll choke on it
if you try to swallow but still

she grinds and grinds. Now it's
Foxtrot, she's sauntering down
the floor, her jaws moving. A
Quickstep begins, she picks

up the pace, chewing, always
chewing—it won't melt, it
won't swallow—until over her
head the stranger is asking,
What are you chewing?
And she answers,

Only my tongue.

THE MASSAGE

They do not lay you, you lay yourself
on the table. They pick up their hands, they
begin to work at the small of your back,
kneading to see if life's still there, deep
buried as a fish under frozen water. They find
the instant of almost-life with pressuring
thumbs, roll it up to the shoulders, raise
it even to the neck, where they settle
it in with their knuckles: this instant

shall not die. And now the dry, knotted neck
is undone by their heel-hands, they toss
tension like horseshoes in some long-ago park,
a harmless evening game; then swipe at
the scalp, set a few hairs quaking,

and pass, remorseless, to the feet. Each
toe's pulled like a tooth, its root cracking,
the horny-skinned pad of the sole is evened
out; what time created is undone, more quickly.

How the ankles ache, coming to life, reluctantly,
how the heart longs to rest hunched under
the sheet. It is not time yet. Now the
restored body must amble up. It will be
a while before the final laying out.

SEVENTEEN: THE PINK DRESS

Coming in on time for once:
        a lamp lit in my mother's bedroom,
her door ajar. She's alone, my
        father's off traveling somewhere.

Sitting up in bed over the parallel lines
        of her legs, in a silk bed jacket,
she calls to me, her voice floating,
        light soprano on the dark

wedge of the house. I go in. She
        motions me down to the side
of her bed—I've never in my life
        sat there—and the wide

blossom of my pink silk dress
        spreads out. She touches it
with a finger, pale emblem
        of what we share: "So pretty"—

the capped sleeves, the modest
        neckline with insert of lace,
fake rosebud pinned at the waist.
        For a moment we sit together

in the inverted bell of light from
        her late lamp, and I know,
this is how she wants me. This is
        how I can never be.

FIRST POEM

It was about fish in a gravelly stream
        in Kentucky, grey shadow fish,
nameless: how they swim
        up toward the tiny waterfall
of a fallen tree; this is not grand.

They told me, right away, that all fish
        are metaphor. I knew that from
the Bible. It wasn't the Bible they
        meant but the abstruse long corridor
that columned my body, that yet

I didn't know. Fish swim up THAT,
        they said, or will, if you're
chosen; even, they hinted, their fish:
        those dark-suited boys who did not wish
to wade in a gravelly Kentucky stream,

their word, their world already weightier
        than my own. So it would be for years,
their words, their smiles channeling my
        words into waterways they counseled

were the world itself, its high banks dim
        and far. I was a good student of their
appreciation, my acquiescence skimmed
        it, they promised me improvement. But the

fish of my first poem, those small
        material bodies, melted like a six-week
fetus, flushed away into other meanings
        as tears, after a while, are only tributes
to what they say we must know.

LEARNING TO SKATE

I was nothing, I was a dull
bird, wingless, dun-brown in my corduroys,
my little white skate-boots belonged
to a doll, Sonja Henji in a pale-pink
dress with a yellow sash; I was
dim, I couldn't stand up, my
ankles leaned in like the two halves
of Plato's egg, and the others

in the class at the Harvard rink
were boarding-school brights from
New England towns whiter than the
Confederacy, and I from the griege
Midwest. They flocked ahead of me,
blades flashing, long legs curved
like the bills of herons, they were
laughing, they knew each other, I was

lying down on the pallid comfort
of the ice. The instructor dragged me
up, she was kind, I was outclassed,
I went on skating all that winter,
1954, carrying my white skates in my

bicycle basket, churning steadily
through class hours toward the
rink. Spring came, the ice didn't thaw,
the herons were still flocking, they
were still laughing. One day
the ice didn't claim me,
one day I looked behind me,
I was skating backwards.

AND YOU WERE THERE
For Candida

And you were there
    on the dim roads of the Normandy town
        just after the war, everything
            still shuttered, everything
                still in short supply,

except for sharp yogurt
    in glass pots topped with cream
        or, in the toyshop
            window, a single
                gleaming sailboat.

A few years later,
    it was "Red Sails
        in the Sunset" for me,
            and you found your
                first boyfriend.

Your mother would never
    approve, you married,
        to please her, a right-
            named stick,
                bore three sons,

spent most of your life
    in bed. Once, on a beach,
        you said, "I'm leaving him,"
            and went for a few days.

When I go to see you now,
        the face of the young
                girl is on the white pillow,

and you are smiling,
        holding out your hand,
                as once on that

Normandy beach, under the
        gun emplacements, you
                smiled and held out
                        your hand for the toy
                                sailboat.

WHERE HE'S STAYING

The name on the codebox
is Travelodge, the number he doesn't
want me to know, his cell
among many others,

brown as dried honey,
where he's staying, socks
and sneakers, the corner
TV's unveiled eye,

all the showers running
together at eight in the morning.
I pray for his comfort there,
in the ordinary lodge

most people are passing
through, but he's staying,
he sees them come and
go, he's friendly with the clerk

at the front desk, pays
his bill on time, they have no
complaints. Somewhere

in his tall torso the seed
that lodged in me thirty
years ago is still planted,
it has sprouted his long
arms, his curl-mad hair;

somewhere in his man's
mouth is the baby mouth
I filled with my milk,

nearly peaceful, rocking
in a chair by a city
window, a New York

spring. When he calls
me to say, Everything's
OK, I don't call back.

I have only the number
on the codebox, the one
he doesn't want me to know.

TELLING TALES

There are no stories now. My grandmother's
legends, lightened up for modernity, die
in a yellowed manuscript, the book she
was so proud of fades on her great-
grandson's shelf. Yet there's something

in my granddaughter's eyes on rainy
city afternoons we don't go out that's
shaped to the shadow of a lost
tale; and when I tell her how the prince—

always the prince—climbed the girl's
long hair without pulling it, then let her
down a ladder like a silk skein, leaving
behind the broken heart of the old witch, a

shattered cup, then I know why these tales
are forbidden, why they still lurk
in the shadows where the old coal furnace
even now winks a treacherous eye.

FIVE

"... only seeming
      to cease when we cease
      to listen."
           —Denise Levertov

Nearly every meal
      one of us
would dip a finger
      in the water inside the crystal glass

and rub the rim
      round and round.
It took a while, but then
      a low hum would begin

to vibrate, and grow. Another
      child began to run
his finger around the rim,
      and a shrill sound, sharper,

joined the hum. Then a third
      started her glass
ringing, and the two youngest
      started, and just for a moment

the joined hum ran
      from glass to
glass around the table and
      just for a moment
we were brothers and sisters together.

MOTHER LOVE

The stranger at the wedding came home to my house where
my two sons slept or didn't sleep. Somehow we managed
to break my bed; I was strangling on laughs, we dragged
the mattress to the floor. We were not done yet, somehow
we were never done and I cannot remember his name
or his face.

Through the wall thin as parchment one son was sleeping
in blue percale pajamas with a white trim; through the
other another son was sleeping or sitting up. We knew
cereal bowls, hot oatmeal, orange juice, the
pediatrician, we knew car seats, seat belts,
inoculations. We did not know the mattress
on the floor.

Let my sons' hearing escape into other meanings,
tie no tin cans to the tail of this tale: the stranger
at the wedding who has no face or name, who comes home
with me, makes me laugh, reaches for the zipper
on my dress;

and my two sons sleeping or not sleeping, who make
their worlds, who do not cry in the morning over
their oatmeal, who do not need to hear me promise,
Never again.

SANNYASA

"I wish to dive into some deep stream of thoughtful
and devoted life. . . ."
        —Thoreau

In the Rogue River backcountry
  of southwestern Oregon, fruit
trees and grape vines grow in a

fenced area; there are no neighbors
  but a small pond. Be prepared
to co-exist with black bears and a

chainsaw, to walk twenty minutes
  by trail to the river, hand crank
the telephone generator, ride high

on the wheels of a four-wheel drive,
  see stars all night. Who's prepared
for the terrible solace of the Dutch Henry

Homestead? For two hours of dust or mud
  to help? For the long spring rains,
the harsh heat of summer? Dutch and

his wife lie under two small stones
  behind the cabin; their dogs
are buried there, too. The new owners

don't visit. You will be asked to sign
  a waiver.

5
DAILY NEWS

CHECHNYA

Trapped too long in the falling city, one way
out for young men always believing in a
way out: Aslambek Ismailor went ahead,
saying, "The women tell me, you live, our sons
die, now I shall go first." Mines bursting
took him, tossed his body into the air,
he fell like a comet, lay scattered in short
grass. The others came on, believing, always
believing, and when the young ones saw
his body scattered, they ran ahead, they
leaped like lovers going to their sweethearts'
beds, they called back, "Meet you in Paradise,"
and the others walked over their bodies
to Alkhan-Kala.

I CANNOT DO
For Will

I cannot do for you what I would do for you
I must stop my heart in its flow
toward you its last drops would not serve
to moisten your lips

I cannot claim to solace you or even
to know where your pain lies or how
waking you look out a small window
toward the light

WALK

Solaced by trees
        by the stream
breaking loose from its ice
        I do not see
the page I do not care
        for its whiteness
it is not the cure
        for blank time

an early thrush
        on top of
a tall tree is music
        to still mine
the light on the
        trail I have walked
so often puts out
        other light

and my hands
        swinging a stick
forget how to shape
        a single word

so God made the world
        and rested

THE TREE THAT GROWS
IN THE CENTER OF THE WORLD

The root of the tree that grows in the center of the
world is what the mother wants from her son,
what she sends him searching for over
the wide seas, through storm and tribulation;
not pearls or brocades or remedies
but that small black root. His voyages go
on and on, whole winters, whole ages
are passing, he pierces the seven seas
while she waits in her chair; and when
he comes in her old age with his knapsack
and spills it into her lap, she sees gold,
she sees rubies, emeralds, she takes them up
in her spotted hands, she does not see what she wants.

SHEARING HIM

The barber has never seen anything like
it, he unlocks his cabinet, he takes out
eight-inch shears, he asks how it
happened—that mat, that mane
no comb can traverse. No answer. The
barber goes to work, his shears clip
majestically, he saws their jaws with
both hands. The mane falls to the floor,
solid, each hair curled and gleaming.
The barber steps over it going for
his clippers, he will not put a toe
in that sea. Afterwards, going out
into the parched light, his head
naked as a sheep's or a newborn's,
my son feels his skull with all
ten fingers.

DAILY NEWS

White as a young tooth,
the new building at Los Alamos
lies on the breakfast table,

a square that fits
        between the newspaper's columns,

built for 98 million
        (less than was asked for)
to house the experiments
of strangers. How can we

in the valley below
        measure?

Also today the pueblo
        to the northwest,
        Santa Clara,

buys back its
        headwaters,
weeps as one

when money comes
        for the reclaiming.

GUACO

My mother's cleome head-high
    sways in her passion's
    garden, its seeds on tender
    stalks vibrate in the

old pueblo house sites,
    proliferate
    in paleofeces,

and mixed with
    iron pigment
    becomes guaco

to paint Rio
    Grande baskets,
    but never so

high-headed
    as my mother's cleome

in the garden
    of her passion.

MAKE-WORK

Passing the piled-up dikes built
across the arroyo by WPA boys sixty
years ago, I look to see whether
the meandering flow of the red dirt
ditch has been upheld or altered:
neither. It follows, still,
its shallow, stubborn course south
to Tesuque Creek, no single turn
or sandbank altered by their labor,
their laid-up alters of stone.

Did those boys, city-bred, breaking
for a lunch of bologna and hard
cheese, wonder about the use
of their handiwork as I,
wandering these dim woods?

So stones
pile up, words pile up, make-
work, cemented with hope, for
the unfolding future where all
work is make-work except
the original act of creation.

SLEEPING IN PEARLS

So many years alone, my body
forgot its language, dropped all
verbs, shrunk nouns to pillow, sheet—
an invalid's lexicon. So I began
to sleep in pearls, a long string,
each white bead cold as death. Like
a swarm of bees they sucked my
nectar all night long, grew
rounder and wiser; like a chain
of daisies, they festooned my
breasts, their touch chilled
my nipples. All that winter
I slept in their chaste embrace,
and somewhere in February, felt
my body speak, felt it forming
the noun for morning,
the verb, to move.

LOSING THE SEXTANT
For John

At evening stars, I went on deck,
searching for Sirius, that old dog,
then mapped my course. Under my hand
three hundred souls slept, safe
as eggs. Now I say, "It was more fun
than anyone has a right to."

Today that sextant, its magic
worn to a shine by two hundred years
sailing the seven seas, slips
from my grasp as circuits heat up,

and the evening stars are cloaked,
their message indistinct. Measured

and measurer fail together.

CROSSING THE BORDER

Before I crossed
the border
I was in no man's
land. She called
me, my love's mother,
and I went
to the zone
where eggs and
butter are reliable
as stars
and thunder
on the horizon
is not howitzers.

After a while
my love took me
back across the
border and all along
the train track
the fields
were silent
although it was August
and the corn
ready for harvest.

THE CHILD WHO

The child who
        once knowing
the benevolence of the universe
        can never unknow it:

the masseur's thumbs
        at the base of her neck
release the lace collar
        of the Elizabethan

lady she was,
        steel
neckband of the
        Etruscan slave—

her, as well—,
        and sliding panes
of time reveal
        only continuity,

no beginnings,
        no ends;
and death,
        when it comes

is only the latest
        proof.

FEBRUARY: LILIES OF THE VALLEY

Spotting a peep of light,
in the packed box,
two pips poke up.

The others wait. In days
to come all, even, face
the light, their roots
spread like dancers'

pale skirts. Advantage is
lost as the sun assaults
equally. Green of the
early starters, their
thrust toward the light,
is reached, then surpassed
by the later pips' uproarious
growth. This sun knows no

favorites, keeps no cracks
for first comers.

EVENT

Flying out of Albuquerque,
        the psychiatrist in his red-
                and-white Cessna spies
                        the far mountains

behind Taos and a storm,
        coming. February. His
                instrument panel glows
                        like Christmas, he's flown

this way often before,
        batting clouds. The lithe
                wings quiver; he climbs;
                        chats on the two-way

with his old-time best friend,
        says, "I'm starting to ice,
                I may be in trouble,"
                        then sets himself to steer

toward the airport lights
        sifting up through
                clouds. After the
                        crash, he walks in the snow

once around the small-boned
        plane. The rescue team
                can't explain how
                        a dead man walked.

But his old friend,
    silent by the chattering
        two-way, knows
            the psychiatrist

who bowed the sky
    between his patients needed
        this last careful check of the
            instrument of his destruction.

THE OLD BURN

On the hillside the old burn
has left its solemn mark: Gambel
Oak, brown-leafed out of season,
stunted pine, carcass of
deciduous tree, unnamable,
on the stark ridge. The past's
ungovernable flame scorches
the green fields of the present,
leaving as marker—" I passed
here"—these survivors,
nor yet the sign, after all
these years, of what the burn
was made for: small green shoots
of a reluctant spring.

BILL CODY'S WILD WEST SHOW

Wild Bill
        wore the costume of the wilderness
all those shows: the Navajo
Third Phase chief blanket,
        red and black,
woven with history,
        the tearing and patching: homespun
wool from sheep wandering the Dinetah,
        commercial yarn
        the railroad brought,
its crossties buffalo bones,
raveled and rewoven flannel
from scarlet fever blankets.

The West,
        for Bill, was a plain
sheet bleached to whiteness
where he and his Indians
could still print hooves,
        then carry the thing
over mountains and seas to a
        credulous people. The

chief blanket seals it, authority
longer than wide, woof of a
Mexico no longer sovereign,
        as the train whistle
        carries the unwilling
        out of the West.

The pretty Virginia widow
dresses her dark hair, dons

her habitual black,
and from the seat of the Deadwood
coach raging round the Richmond ring,
      he spies her,

set like the sunflower's dark core
      in her radiating family, and
plucks, or seeks to pluck, her.
Next day, after
church, she's permitted
a modest edgewood ride with
      the wild man,
permits herself to leap down
from the sidesaddle into his arms,

and, for a moment, before propriety
      claims her,
claims her for the rest of her long life,
she brushes the mixed fibers
of the Navajo chief blanket with
her bare arm. What more
      can life offer?

To know, before change and drudgery,
      the brief touch
of Dineh wool and eastern yarn,
      dangerous softness
of germ-soaked flannel and
then, unscathed, withdraw
      her arm.

> Later,
> she receives his first and
> last gift: a silver-handled riding
> crop, lady-sized, but with a smart
> > snap.

SUNDAY AFTERNOON CONCERT

In the Mexican madhouse
naked men and women—
"He wasn't quite in his
music," someone says of the
visiting first violin—walk
in their shit, shaped
like the necks of cellos,
and when the Norte Americano
doctor says, "They're not
human," then speaks to one—
"She has a story"—, it's like
when the blond imported violinist
flings up his bow arm, radiant,
fresh, exulting to the rest,
"It is accomplished"—to
the tired, obliged faces of
the third-rate, the always deceived,
and the flat hand that matches
the flat face of the mongoloid
boy in the audience creeps, again,
across his mother's back, and at
the same moment the naked inmates
of the Mexican madhouse are herded
unwashed to their evening meal.

After intermission, the somewhat
disheveled players in the provincial
orchestra return, one young man
tootles his trumpet, and now a
father carries his daughter
sidesaddle on his hip to see

the instruments still lying
on their sides like cows
in a field; and the burly
cellist swipes his face
with a red towel, and the
inmates of the Mexican madhouse
are still returning, naked, from
their evening meal to the
square concrete cell
where together, seventy or so,
they will be hosed down.

Will music clothe these bones?
Can the tear-draining
sweetness of the silver
clarinet wash clean
these abandoned limbs,
or the tootling trumpet trouble
heaven for their relief? Still
the mother of the mongoloid
boy soothes him, still the father
carries his drowsy daughter
back to their seats, still
love and the world go on.

NOW WE ARE THIRTY
For Will

It's so cold the single apple
in the bowl on my windowsill
wrinkles, so cold the wood stove pushes
against a rectangle of iced air,
and you are thirty today and I am
thirty, remembering the delivery table,
the short, terrible struggle (once already
in blood drops you'd tried to leave me),
and afterwards when the doctor and nurses
were cleaning you—calm, still,
already looking around you—, I lay
torn by that struggle, empty
as a hollowed-out heart on that
steel table, and my body spoke
with a voice unheard till then,
saying, "This is enough."

Now you are thirty and further
from me. Your telephone's disconnected,
I don't know your address. All those
presents—stuffed animals, books,
clothes that never quite fit—have
shredded into this silence.
I do not know who you are. Perhaps
I have never known who you are.

The chill weight of this lightless air
presses its lid down on me, seals
tears, seals questions, seals
complaints. This is the way it is.
This is the way it has always been.
I give praise to the angels
that you are still alive.

DEATH OF MEDICINE WHEEL

Black her first phrase,
born to prophesy,
to testify,
the buffalo calf
flows free through the
gate leaned back.

Red her second phase,
not to be achieved,
yellowish-white
also denied,
final white of
absolution.

She flows down the
reservation road,
property of one,
of all.

Dusk. The sheriff
in fear sights her,
shoots her to protect
his people.

So Crazy Horse,
bayonet in his breast,
saw the secret
cave of his burial,
said, "They tried
to contain me."

Shut the gate.
Lay up the rifle.
Medicine Wheel still
turns through her
four colors, still unites

the desperate, the disparate.

SISTERS-IN-LAW

Not in the rich valley
    but on the rocky side
    of a nameless hill,
I speak to you,
you speak to me.

I remember you,
    dark-eyed bride,
    trembling, laughing,
you remember me,
    blue-eyed bride,
    always in tears.

The years don't roll away.
They squat like boulders.
    Under each one
    a dark patch,
    always a little damp,

the bowed heads
of newly-sprouted seeds.

Book design by Vicki Ahl.
This book of poetry has been printed on acid free paper.
The typeface is Adobe Garamond Pro.
♣

www.ingramcontent.com/pod-product-compliance
Lightning Source LLC
Chambersburg PA
CBHW021018090426
42738CB00007B/814